IRISH COOKING

Ruth Bauder Kershner

WEATHERVANE
BOOKS

contents

introduction

Ireland is a country of rolling green farmlands, heavy mists, and rugged seacoast. It is picturesque, preserving a bit of the past in its thatch-roofed cottages and smoking chimneys.

Hospitality is an integral part of the Irish personality. Both friend and stranger are greeted with a soft-spoken "Cead mille failte," which means "a hundred thousand welcomes." A bounteous table is spread. The food is prepared with loving care in the ways learned by every daughter from her mother. It is hearty and generally simple in preparation, to accentuate the fresh, full flavor of quality foods produced by an agricultural nation. Nearly one-third of the work force of Ireland is employed in agriculture. The land, in addition to its great beauty, yields a heavy bounty. The mainstays of the Irish diet are the home-grown, the home-reared, and the homemade. The food tends to be high in caloric content and is intended to satisfy even the heartiest working man.

Many of the foods still present in the Irish diet have their roots in ancient times. Oatmeal was first used by the Celts, and oatmeal porridge is still a breakfast staple of the Irish population. The Saxons introduced spices to all those they conquered: ginger, cloves, nutmeg, and cinnamon were introduced into the cuisine. Even though potatoes are associated with the Irish, they were brought to Ireland by the English, and were not heavily propagated until the eighteenth century. Deep Catholic roots in the South of Ireland have heavily influenced the diet, with special foods planned around religious feasts and the fast days preceding them.

Meat is a staple of the Irish diet. Beef, pork, and lamb are the preferred meats—prepared in soups and stews or served as roasts and chops. Organ meats are not disdained; in fact, tripe and onions is considered a great delicacy. Bacon and hams are home-cured and delicious. Chicken as well as duck and goose are roasted for Sunday dinner. Hunting is a favorite Irish pastime, and game is prepared in season. Ireland has many lakes and streams, with salmon and trout abounding. Fish is generally simply prepared, highlighting its delicious flavor. Salmon and trout are also smoked and thinly sliced and served as a first course. Being an island nation, Ireland makes good use of the rich bounty the surrounding ocean provides. Oysters, crab, and lobster as well as all types of ocean fish are eaten.

Potatoes are indeed the backbone of Irish cooking. They are boiled in their jackets, baked, mashed, fried, and even used in breads and cakes. Other vegetables are eaten in season, with a heavy emphasis on the root vegetables such as carrots, onions, and turnips, which have excellent keeping qualities. Cabbage, onions, and beets are pickled for winter use and provide an excellent foil for boiled meats.

A variety of fruits are grown, with apples, lemons, plums, pears, and peaches being especially favored. These fruits form the basis for beautiful cakes and tarts and delicious preserves and jams for winter use.

Baking has been elevated to a fine Irish art, with homemade breads served at every meal. Soda bread is indeed a touch of Irish genius. A crisp, crusted, biscuit-like loaf is ready to eat in a matter of minutes.

Being an agricultural country, the Irish use dairy products in their cookery. Butter is used, rather than margarine or oil, in most cooking. The milk used is generally buttermilk or sour milk, since refrigeration was not widely available in Ireland until recent years. Cheese-making is a relatively young industry in Ireland, and cheese is used infrequently in cooking.

Eating is usually a bounteous and leisurely family activity in Ireland. Breakfast is a large meal, generally eaten early. Oatmeal porridge is usually eaten accompanied by fresh eggs, smokey bacon, homemade bread, butter, and preserves. Strong black tea with milk and sugar is served with all meals. The midday meal is usually the main meal of the day, eaten at home with the whole family. A hearty soup, followed by meat, potatoes, vegetable, bread, and dessert, provides a substantial diet for the hard-working farmer. The late-afternoon to early-evening meal is referred to as "tea." In Great Britain, it might be called "meat tea," since eggs and light meat dishes such as meat pies and salmon cakes are served in addition to cakes, breads, and tea. In urban areas tea is a late afternoon ladies' affair with tea and cakes, and supper is served later in the evening.

A word about Irish potables is in order here. Tea is extremely important to the Irish. It is served at all times of the day. It is a dark brew made from fermented black teas, usually from Ceylon or Africa. It is served fresh and hot with milk and sugar and provides excellent warmth against the dense Irish mists. Guiness stout, with its creamy head of foam, can indeed be called the Irish drink. It is strong in flavor and dark in color. It should not be chilled but served at room temperature. Porter is a slightly lighter drink, favored in the north of Ireland. Last, we come to the king of Irish potables—Irish whiskey. It is pot-still whiskey, generally aged seven years in wood. It is drunk "neat" (straight) or with only a little water. Ice cubes are considered sacrilege, spoiling the honest character of the whiskey. Irish Mist is a liqueur made from Dew whiskey and is quite delicious with coffee. Whiskey and stout are enjoyed with much conversation and comaraderie in the Irish pubs. Here the men congregate, and this is surely where the Irish "gift of the gab" originated.

Irish food is best known for the quality of its ingredients and the honesty of its preparation. It is satisfying and delightful to the palate. I hope you will enjoy the following recipes and glimpse in them a hint of the Irish character.

soups and starters

hough soup

A hearty beef and vegetable soup.

stock

3 pounds sliced beef shin
1 pound beef bones (split marrow bone or neck bone)
1 onion, studded with 4 cloves
1 bay leaf
½ teaspoon crumbled dried thyme

1 cup broken-up canned tomatoes
1 stalk celery (including some leaves), chopped
¼ cup chopped parsley
2 teaspoons salt
10 cups water

soup

1 turnip, peeled, diced
1 large onion, thinly sliced
3 large carrots, peeled, sliced
2 stalks celery, sliced
1 16-ounce can tomatoes, broken up

¼ cup chopped parsley
¼ medium cabbage head, shredded
½ cup long-grain rice

The day before serving: Place beef shin and bones in shallow roasting pan. Roast in 400°F oven until browned. Place in Dutch oven with remaining stock ingredients. Bring to boil; skim if necessary. Cover with lid ajar; simmer 3 to 4 hours or until meat falls from bones. Remove meat; cool. Strain stock; refrigerate. Remove bones and any fat and gristle from meat; dice. Reserve meat for soup.

The following day: Combine stock, reserved meat, and soup ingredients in large Dutch oven or soup kettle. Bring to boil; cover. Reduce heat to low; cook 40 to 50 minutes, or until vegetables and rice are tender. Makes 8 servings.

cottage broth

This soup makes a whole meal in itself, served with assorted hot breads, sliced cheese, and a green salad.

stock

2 lamb shanks (about 3 pounds)	2 teaspoons salt
7 cups water	4 peppercorns
1 onion, studded with 4 cloves	2 carrots, peeled, chopped
2 bay leaves	1 stalk celery, chopped

soup

3 tablespoons butter or margarine	2 stalks celery, chopped
2 leeks, cleaned, sliced	¼ cup chopped parsley
1 medium onion, chopped	1 teaspoon crumbled dried thyme
2 turnips, peeled, diced	¼ cup barley, soaked overnight
3 medium carrots, peeled, sliced	in water to cover

The day before serving: Place lamb shanks in shallow roasting pan; roast at 400°F until well-browned (20 to 30 minutes). Place lamb and remaining stock ingredients in Dutch oven. Bring to boil. Cover; reduce heat to low. Simmer 2½ to 3 hours or until meat is very tender. Remove meat from broth. Strain stock. Discard vegetables. Refrigerate stock overnight. Remove lamb from shanks; dice. Reserve for soup.

The following day: Melt butter or margarine in large Dutch oven. Add vegetables, except parsley; cook over moderate heat, stirring occasionally, until tender.

Remove fat from soup stock; add to vegetables. Add parsley, thyme, barley (drained), and reserved lamb; mix well. Bring soup to boil; cover. Reduce heat to low; cook 1 to 1¼ hours or until barley is tender. Makes 8 servings.

craibechan of the sea

"Craibechan" means any savory mixture of little bits and pieces.

3 tablespoons butter
1 clove garlic, peeled, chopped
1 leek, cleaned, sliced
1 medium onion, peeled, chopped
3 cups cooked seafood (Lobster, crab, and shrimp can be used, or salmon and cod make a good combination. Steam or poach fish; cool.)
Salt and pepper
Few drops of Tabasco
1 small head Bibb lettuce
1 lemon, cut into wedges
Radish roses

Melt butter in small skillet. Add garlic, leek, and onion; sauté until tender. Combine onion mixture and seafood; pass through food chopper. Season with salt, pepper, and Tabasco to taste. Refrigerate until serving time.

Line plates with Bibb lettuce; mound fish mixture in center of plate. Garnish with lemon wedges and radish roses. Makes 4 servings.

split-pea soup with crubeens

2 cups split peas
Cold water
2 pigs' feet, split
½ cup chopped onion
1 cup chopped celery
½ cup chopped carrot
1 medium potato, peeled, chopped
1 bay leaf
1 teaspoon salt
¼ teaspoon crumbled dried thyme
Dash cayenne pepper
2 tablespoons butter
2 tablespoons flour

fried croutons
2 slices thick white bread
2 tablespoons butter
  or margarine

Rinse peas; pick over. Place in bowl; cover with water. Soak overnight. Drain any remaining liquid from peas; add water to make 10 cups of liquid. Combine peas and liquid in Dutch oven.

Rinse pigs' feet under running water; add to peas. Bring to boil. Skim any foam. Reduce heat to low; cook 1½ to 2 hours. Remove pigs' feet. Add vegetables and seasonings; cook 1 hour more. When pigs' feet have cooled, remove skin and bones; chop meat. Puree soup in electric blender or pass through sieve. Add chopped meat.

Melt butter in small saucepan. Add flour; cook until bubbly. Add small amount of soup to flour mixture, stirring well. Pour back into soup kettle. Stir well; cook 5 minutes.

Next make croutons. Remove crusts from bread; cut into ½-inch cubes. Melt butter in heavy skillet; fry bread cubes over moderate heat until golden. Drain; serve sprinkled on soup. Makes 6 to 8 servings.

cream of potato soup

3 tablespoons butter or margarine
1 cup chopped onion
1 cup chopped celery
4 cups peeled, diced potatoes
1 10¾-ounce can chicken broth
1 soup-can water
1 13-ounce can evaporated milk
2 tablespoons flour
Chopped chives or crisp bacon for garnish

Melt butter or margarine in large saucepan. Sauté onion and celery until onion is transparent. Add potatoes, chicken broth, and water. Bring to boil. Reduce heat to low; cook, covered, 40 to 45 minutes or until vegetables are very tender. Puree soup in electric blender until smooth, or force through sieve. Return to saucepan. Add milk, reserving ¼ cup. Simmer 20 minutes.

Combine flour with reserved milk, mixing well. Add to soup; cook, stirring constantly, until soup is thick and creamy.

Serve soup hot, garnished with chopped chives or crisp bacon curls. Makes 6 to 8 servings.

Note: The flour can be omitted if a thinner soup is desired.

aran scallop soup

This soup is a specialty of the Aran Islands.

fish stock

1½ pounds small fish, cleaned, or fish trimmings (heads, tails, and
    bones of mild ocean fish, or lobster and shrimp shells)
3 cups cold water
½ cup chopped onion
¼ cup chopped carrot
½ cup chopped celery
½ cup white wine
1 bay leaf
3 peppercorns
Several parsley sprigs
1 cup clam juice

soup

¾ pound fresh scallops
2 slices bacon, diced
2 cups peeled, diced potatoes
½ teaspoon salt
¼ teaspoon white pepper
1 tablespoon chopped parsley
½ teaspoon crumbled dried thyme
2 cups peeled diced tomatoes
1½ cups hot light cream
¾ cup crushed water biscuits or pilot crackers
Pats of butter
Ground mace
Chopped parsley

First make fish stock. Wash fish or trimmings in cold water; drain. Combine water, vegetables, and wine in heavy saucepan. Tie bay leaf, peppercorns, and parsley in small piece of cheesecloth; add seasonings and fish or trimmings to water and vegetables. Bring to boil over moderate heat; cook uncovered 20 to 30 minutes. Strain stock; add clam juice. Reserve.

Next prepare soup. Wash scallops in cold water. If large, cut in half or quarter. Drain; reserve. Sauté bacon in large, heavy saucepan 3 to 4 minutes or until it starts to brown. Add potatoes; cook until tender. Add salt, pepper, parsley, thyme, tomatoes, and reserved fish stock. Stir well; cook over moderate heat 15 minutes. Add scallops; bring to gentle boil. Cover; reduce heat to low. Cook 10 to 12 minutes or until scallops are cooked through.

Stir in heated cream. Do not allow mixture to boil after adding cream. Slowly stir in water biscuits, while cooking over low heat, to thicken soup.

Ladle soup into bowls; float a pat of butter on each serving. Garnish with chopped parsley and a sprinkling of mace. Makes 4 servings.

balnamoon skink

2½- to 3-pound chicken
6 cups water
2 teaspoons salt
½ teaspoon pepper
1 celery root
1 leek, sliced
1 large carrot, peeled, sliced
2 tablespoons chopped parsley
1¼ cups frozen peas
¼ teaspoon ground mace
2 egg yolks
½ cup whipping cream
2 cups shredded leaf lettuce or outer leaves of an iceberg lettuce

Wash chicken well inside and out. Combine chicken, water, salt, and pepper in Dutch oven. Cover; bring to boil over moderate heat. Skim any scum from surface. Reduce heat to low; cook 1 hour.

Clean and cube celery root. Add celery root, leek, and carrot to soup; cook 15 minutes. Remove chicken; cool slightly. Skin; remove from bones; dice. Return chicken to soup. Add parsley, peas, and mace; simmer 8 to 10 minutes.

Beat egg yolks and cream together well in small bowl. Add some of soup to cream mixture; beat well. Add slowly to soup, mixing well. Cook over very low heat 3 minutes.

Ladle soup into serving bowls; sprinkle each bowl with some lettuce. Makes 6 servings.

cured trout

Smoked or cured salmon or trout is a traditional Irish appetizer. It is served very thinly sliced against the grain and served on lettuce with lemon wedges. Irish smoked salmon is truly a delicacy, but very expensive! Try the following version of cured trout as a substitute. Start early, as this recipe takes 7 days to make.

1 4-pound trout (or 2 2-pound trout), boned, butterflied, head removed
4½ teaspoons salt
½ teaspoon freshly ground pepper
½ teaspoon garlic powder
6 tablespoons olive oil
1 tablespoon brown sugar

On the day you begin the curing process, wash fish; pat dry with paper towels. Place on large nonmetallic platter. Combine salt and seasonings; place in a small shaker bottle. On day 1 rub fish with ⅓ of salt mixture. Cover with plastic wrap; refrigerate.

On day 2 drain any liquid from platter; rub fish with 2 tablespoons oil. Cover; refrigerate overnight.

Rub fish with salt mixture on days 3 and 5 and with oil on days 4 and 6.

On day 6 also rub fish with sugar.

On day 7 hang fish in cool, dry, breezy place 24 hours. Then, to serve, slice paper thin against the grain. Makes 10 to 12 appetizer servings.

10

*balnamoon
skink*

*oysters on the half shell and
dublin prawn cocktail*

oysters on the half shell

24 oysters
Beds of lettuce or crushed ice
Lemon wedges
Tabasco sauce

Wash oysters well to remove sand and grit.

Prepare beds of lettuce or crushed ice.

Open oysters with oyster knife just before serving. Discard top shell; loosen oyster from bottom of shell by cutting ligaments.

Serve oysters immediately. Garnish with lemon wedges; accompany with Tabasco. Pass lots of whole-wheat soda bread. Makes 4 servings.

dublin prawn cocktail

1 pound large shrimp or prawns
½ cup water
½ cup vinegar

2 teaspoons seafood seasoning
1 teaspoon salt
⅛ teaspoon garlic powder

Wash shrimp under cold running water; drain.

Combine water, vinegar, seafood seasoning, salt, and garlic in large saucepan; bring to boil. Add shrimp; stir well. Return to boil; cover. Reduce heat to low; cook approximately 10 minutes or until shrimp are pink and firm. Drain; rinse in cold water. Peel and devein shrimp, leaving last joint of tail intact.

Arrange shrimp on bed of Bibb lettuce or on bed of crushed ice. Serve with Dublin Cocktail Sauce. Makes 3 to 4 servings.

dublin cocktail sauce
¼ cup tomato catsup
¼ cup whipping cream
1½ tablespoons prepared horseradish
½ teaspoon lemon juice

Combine all ingredients; mix well. Chill until serving time.

12

cock-a-leekie soup

This soup was served frequently in medieval times, when it was customarily garnished with prunes stuffed with hazelnuts.

½ cup pearl barley
1 2- to 3-pound chicken
1 veal knuckle (approximately ¾ pound)
2 quarts water

2 teaspoons salt
1 bay leaf
6 peppercorns
3 sprigs parsley
6 leeks (approximately 1 pound)

Cover barley with cold water; soak 12 hours.

Rinse chicken inside and out; pat dry. Combine chicken, veal knuckle, 2 quarts water, and salt in large pot.

Tie bay leaf, peppercorns, and parsley in piece of cheesecloth; add to soup kettle.

Drain barley; add to other ingredients. Bring to boil over high heat; skim foam from soup. Reduce heat to moderate; cook 1½ hours.

Meanwhile, clean and slice leeks; add to soup.

Remove chicken; cool. Remove veal knuckle; discard.

Cook soup 30 minutes more. When chicken is cool enough to handle, skin it; remove meat from bones. Cut into 1-inch pieces; return to soup.

Remove and discard cheesecloth bag of seasonings. Taste soup; add salt and pepper if necessary. Makes 4 to 6 servings.

dublin clam soup

Traditionally this soup would be made with cockles or mussels, which can be substituted for clams if available.

3 dozen clams
1 cup water
1 medium onion, chopped
1 bay leaf
2 tablespoons chopped parsley
3 tablespoons sweet butter
3 tablespoons flour

2 cups milk
½ cup heavy cream
1 egg yolk
¼ teaspoon nutmeg
Salt and white pepper to taste
Chopped parsley

Scrub clams well; wash in cold running water to remove sand. Discard any clams with open or damaged shells.

Combine the water, onion, bay leaf, and parsley in large saucepan. Add clams; cover; bring to boil. Reduce heat to low; cook 5 to 10 minutes or until shells open. Remove clams from shells; reserve. If desired, discard only top shells, then place clams in soup bowl with bottom shell intact. Strain broth; reserve.

Melt butter in heavy saucepan. Add flour; cook until bubbly. Add milk; cook, stirring constantly, until thick. Add clam broth; heat through.

Beat cream and egg yolk together; add some of hot soup to mixture. Beat well; add to saucepan. Cook over low heat, stirring constantly, 3 minutes. Add nutmeg and salt and pepper to taste. Stir in clams. Heat 1 to 2 minutes. Serve immediately. Makes 4 to 6 servings.

fish and egg dishes

creamed fresh haddock

1 pound fresh haddock fillets (or other firm white-fish fillets)
½ cup melted butter or margarine
Flour
½ cup slivered onion
Salt and pepper
1 cup light cream
½ teaspoon dry mustard

Wash fillets; pat dry. Dip fillets in melted butter; dredge in flour. Arrange in shallow baking dish in single layer. Arrange onion on top of fish. Sprinkle with salt and pepper. Add cream; top with any remaining butter. Bake in preheated 350°F oven 20 to 25 minutes or until fish flakes easily with fork. Baste with pan juices several times during cooking. Remove fish from baking dish; keep warm.

Stir dry mustard into cream mixture in baking dish. Taste sauce; add salt and pepper if necessary. Pour sauce over fish.

Serve fish garnished with chopped parsley and sprinkled lightly with paprika. Makes 4 servings.

poached cod with lemon sauce

1 pound cod fillets
Seasoned salt and pepper
1 tablespoon lemon juice
2 shallots, peeled, chopped
¼ cup white wine
1 tablespoon butter or margarine

lemon sauce
1 tablespoon butter or margarine
¾ cup mayonnaise
Juice of ½ lemon
½ teaspoon dry mustard
½ teaspoon salt
½ tablespoon capers, drained, chopped

Wash fish; pat dry. Sprinkle with salt, pepper, and 1 tablespoon lemon juice. Place in small, greased casserole dish. Sprinkle with shallots; pour wine over all. Dot with 1 tablespoon butter; cover. Bake at 350°F 20 to 25 minutes or until fish flakes easily with fork.

Meanwhile, melt 1 tablespoon butter in top of double boiler. Add remaining sauce ingredients, except capers. Cook, stirring constantly, over simmering water until heated through. Stir in capers.

Place fish on a heated platter and top with the sauce. Serve immediately, garnished with lemon slices. Makes 4 servings.

poached salmon with egg sauce

1 quart water
½ lemon, sliced
½ cup white wine
¼ cup sliced onion
1 bay leaf
4 peppercorns
1 teaspoon salt
4 small salmon steaks (approximately 4 ounces each)

egg sauce
3 tablespoons butter or margarine
1 tablespoon finely chopped onion
1 tablespoon finely chopped green pepper
1½ tablespoons flour
⅓ cup broth in which fish was cooked
¾ cup milk
½ teaspoon dry mustard
Salt and pepper
2 hard-cooked eggs, chopped

Combine water, lemon, wine, ¼ cup onion, bay leaf, peppercorns, and 1 teaspoon salt in heavy skillet; bring to boil.

Wrap salmon steaks in cheesecloth; secure. Place in boiling stock; cover. Reduce heat to low; cook 10 minutes. Drain; keep warm while making sauce.

Melt 3 tablespoons butter in small saucepan. Add 1 tablespoon onion and green pepper; sauté 3 minutes. Add flour; cook, stirring constantly, until bubbly. Stir in fish stock, milk, mustard, salt, and pepper; cook, stirring constantly, until thickened. Stir in eggs. Serve. Makes 4 servings.

cocklety pie

An excellent shellfish pie!

pastry crust

1 cup all-purpose flour
½ teaspoon salt
3 tablespoons cold butter
2 to 3 tablespoons cold water

scallop and mushroom filling

1 pound sea scallops
½ cup white wine
1 cup water
3 chopped shallots (green onions can be substituted)
1 bay leaf
2 peppercorns
1 cup peeled, diced potatoes
1 6½-ounce can button mushrooms
2 tablespoons chopped parsley
3 tablespoons butter
3 tablespoons flour
¼ teaspoon dry mustard
Salt and pepper
1 cup light cream
¾ cup reserved fish stock

1 egg yolk
1 tablespoon milk

First make pastry for crust. Combine flour and salt, mixing well. Cut butter into flour until mixture resembles coarse cornmeal. Blend water into flour mixture a tablespoon at a time while mixing with fork, just until moistened. Gather into ball; wrap in plastic wrap. Refrigerate while making Scallop and Mushroom Filling.

Wash scallops under cold running water to remove sand and grit. Halve or quarter scallops if large.

Combine wine, water, shallots, bay leaf, and peppercorns in medium saucepan. Bring to boil over moderate heat. Add scallops; cover. Reduce heat to low; cook 10 minutes.

Meanwhile, cook potatoes in small saucepan of salted water until tender. Drain; reserve.

Drain scallops; reserve cooking liquid. Combine scallops, potatoes, mushrooms, and parsley in lightly greased 1½-quart casserole. Mix well; set aside.

Melt butter in heavy saucepan. Add flour, mustard, salt, and pepper; cook, stirring constantly, until bubbly. Add cream and ¾ cup reserved fish broth (strained); cook over low heat, stirring constantly, until mixture thickens. Pour over fish and mushrooms in casserole; mix well.

Roll pastry crust on lightly floured board to fit top of casserole. Place crust over fish mixture; turn edges under; flute. Reroll any scraps; use to make leaves or other decorations. Beat egg yolk and milk together; brush crust well. Bake in preheated 425°F oven 20 to 30 minutes or until crust is golden brown. Serve hot. Makes 4 servings.

16

haddock and potato bake

1 pound potatoes (approximately 3 medium potatoes)
Water
½ teaspoon salt
1 pound haddock fillets, thawed if frozen
4 tablespoons butter or margarine
2 medium onions, peeled, sliced
Salt and pepper
1 egg yolk
⅔ cup sour cream
¼ teaspoon ground mace
⅓ cup dry bread crumbs
1 tablespoon melted butter or margarine
Paprika
Dried parsley flakes

Peel potatoes; cover with cold water. Add salt; cover; bring to boil. Reduce heat to low; cook 15 to 20 minutes or until fork-tender. Drain. Place tea towel over pan; steam over very low heat 5 minutes. Cool slightly.

Cut haddock into 1-inch squares; pat dry with paper towels.

Slice potatoes.

Melt butter in heavy saucepan; sauté onions until lightly browned.

Lightly grease 1½-quart casserole. Place ⅓ of potatoes in casserole; sprinkle with salt and pepper. Top with ½ of haddock and ½ of onion and butter mixture. Top with ⅓ of potatoes, salt, pepper, and remaining haddock and onion mixture. Top with remaining potatoes.

Combine egg yolk, sour cream, and mace; spread over top layer of potatoes.

Combine bread crumbs and melted butter; sprinkle over casserole. Dust lightly with paprika and parsley flakes. Bake at 350°F 30 to 40 minutes or until top is golden brown. Makes 4 servings.

egg collops

1 tablespoon butter
1 tablespoon finely chopped onion
2 tablespoons finely chopped green pepper
4 large hard-boiled eggs, chopped
½ cup cream of celery soup
Salt and pepper
Flour
1 egg, well-beaten
2 tablespoons water
Fine dry bread crumbs
Oil for deep frying

Melt butter in small saucepan. Add onion and green pepper; sauté until tender.

Combine eggs, vegetable mixture, soup, salt, and pepper in mixing bowl; mix well. Form into 8 croquettes. Dredge lightly in flour.

Beat egg with 2 tablespoons water. Dip croquettes in egg wash, then in bread crumbs. Pat so that bread crumbs adhere thickly to croquettes.

Heat oil in deep fryer to 365°F. Fry croquettes 2 at a time until golden. Drain well. Serve. Makes 4 servings.

potato omelet

4 slices bacon
1½ cups peeled, thinly sliced potatoes
½ cup finely chopped onion
¼ cup finely chopped green pepper
4 eggs
Salt and pepper

Cook bacon in heavy skillet until crisp. Drain; crumble; reserve.

Add potatoes to hot bacon fat in skillet; sauté 5 minutes or until potatoes are just tender. Add onion and green pepper; sauté 3 minutes.

Beat eggs with salt and pepper; pour over potatoes in skillet. Sprinkle with bacon; cook over medium heat as you would an omelet, without stirring, until eggs begin to set. Cover; cook a few minutes longer, until eggs are completely set and bottom of omelet is browned.

Serve omelet cut in wedges, garnished with parsley and tomato wedges. Makes 2 servings.

potatoes stuffed with corned beef

4 medium baking potatoes
4 tablespoons butter or margarine
¼ cup finely minced onion
¼ cup finely minced green pepper
2 to 3 tablespoons milk
1 teaspoon Worcestershire sauce
1 cup chopped canned corned beef
Salt and pepper
3 cups water
1 teaspoon salt
2 teaspoons vinegar
4 eggs
Minced parsley

Scrub potatoes well; prick with fork in several places. Bake at 375°F 1 to 1¼ hours or until easily pierced with fork.

Meanwhile, melt 2 tablespoons butter in small saucepan. Sauté onion and green pepper until tender.

When potatoes are cool enough to handle, remove thin slice from top of each potato. Scoop out inside of potato, leaving ¼-inch-thick shell. Place potato pulp in mixing bowl with remaining 2 tablespoons butter. Beat, adding enough milk to make stiff mashed-potato mixture. Add Worcestershire sauce, corned beef, onion, green pepper, and butter in which they were cooked; mix well. Add salt and pepper to taste. Fill potato shells with mixture, making a well in top of each potato. Bake at 350°F 30 minutes.

Meanwhile, combine water and 1 teaspoon salt in medium saucepan; bring to boil. Add vinegar to boiling water. Break eggs, 1 at a time, into sauce dish; slide into boiling water. Poach eggs to desired degree of doneness.

Place 1 poached egg in well on top of each potato. Garnish with parsley. Serve. Makes 4 servings.

Note: The stuffed potatoes can be prepared a day in advance and refrigerated until baking time. Allow a few extra minutes to heat.

dressed crab

1 pound cooked crab meat
2 tablespoons butter
1 cup fresh bread crumbs
½ cup whipping cream, lightly whipped
1 tablespoon lemon juice
1 tablespoon finely minced green onion
1 teaspoon Worcestershire sauce
½ teaspoon dry mustard
Few drops of Tabasco
Salt and pepper
2 tablespoons melted butter
Parsley flakes and paprika

Lightly grease 4 natural crab shells, if available, or use 4 small ovenproof ramekins.

Pick over crab meat, discarding any bits of shell and cartilage.

Melt 2 tablespoons butter in heavy skillet; heat until lightly browned. Add crab meat; toss well. Combine crab and remaining ingredients, except 2 tablespoons melted butter, parsley flakes, and paprika. Mix lightly but thoroughly. Place in shells or ramekins. Drizzle with melted butter; sprinkle with parsley flakes and paprika. Place on baking sheet; bake at 375°F 15 minutes or until lightly browned. Serve hot. Makes 4 servings.

dressed crab

grilled salmon with lemon butter

grilled salmon with lemon butter

lemon butter
¼ cup butter (½ stick), room temperature
1 tablespoon chopped fresh parsley
1 small shallot, finely chopped
½ tablespoon lemon juice

grilled salmon
4 salmon steaks, 1 inch thick
2 tablespoons melted butter
1 tablespoon lemon juice
1 tablespoon chopped fresh dill or ½ teaspoon dried dillweed

Make Lemon Butter at least 8 hours in advance of serving. (It can be prepared and refrigerated at least 1 month before use.) Combine all ingredients for flavored butter; beat with electric mixer until well-blended. Place on piece of plastic wrap; form into 3 × 3-inch square, using spatula. Wrap with plastic wrap; refrigerate.

Light standard charcoal barbecue fire. When fire has burned down and coals are glowing, place salmon steaks on grill.

Combine melted butter, lemon juice, and dill; brush steaks well with mixture. Grill approximately 12 minutes (6 to 7 minutes per side), turning once and basting with butter mixture. Remove from grill.

Divide Lemon Butter into 4 pats; place 1 pat on each salmon steak. Serve immediately. Makes 4 servings.

20

bacon and eggs

bacon and eggs

½ pound thickly sliced bacon (country-cured if available)
4 (or more) large eggs
Salt and pepper

Trim rind from bacon. Fry in large, heavy skillet until crisp, 4 to 5 slices at a time. Keep warm. Pour off all fat; reserve.

Clean pan with paper towels, removing all browned bits. Pour 6 tablespoons fat into pan. Heat over moderate heat until few drops of water dance in fat. Break eggs into fat, 1 at a time. Reduce heat to low; cook until whites begin to set. Baste yolks with hot bacon fat by tipping pan and spooning hot fat over yolks. Cook until whites are set and yolks are still soft, but glazed over in appearance.

Serve eggs immediately with bacon, hot mashed potato cakes, and freshly made toast.

sunday morning omelet

2 tablespoons butter or margarine
4 medium eggs, lightly beaten
Salt and pepper
½ cup chopped baked ham
1 tablespoon chopped chives
1 tablespoon chopped parsley

Melt butter in 10-inch skillet.

Meanwhile, beat eggs with salt and pepper to taste. Pour egg mixture into skillet; cook over low heat without stirring. As eggs cook, lift edges of omelet; allow uncooked egg to flow to bottom of pan. When eggs are set, loosen from pan; sprinkle with ham, chives, and parsley. Fold in half; heat through.

Slide omelet onto platter; garnish with parsley and sliced tomatoes. Serve with potato cakes. Makes 2 servings.

21

eggs wrapped in ham

8 thick slices bacon
4 slices boiled ham
4 large hard-boiled eggs, shelled
1 8-ounce can tomato sauce
½ teaspoon sweet basil
Salt and pepper
2 tablespoons melted butter
Parsley for garnish

Fry bacon in heavy skillet until lightly browned but not crisp. Drain on paper towels.

Cut ham slices in half; trim so that pieces are same size as bacon.

Slice hard-boiled eggs in half lengthwise.

Place 1 slice of ham on slice of bacon; wrap around outside of 1 hard-boiled-egg half. Secure with toothpick. Follow same procedure with remaining egg halves. Place in 8- or 9-inch-square baking dish or equivalent, yolk facing up.

Combine tomato sauce, sweet basil, salt, and pepper; mix well. Pour around egg halves. Brush exposed egg yolks and white with melted butter. Bake eggs at 350°F 20 minutes.

Serve eggs on toast with sauce spooned over. Makes 4 servings.

eggs wrapped in ham

22

meat, poultry, and game

beef 'n beer stew

3 tablespoons flour
¾ teaspoon salt
¼ teaspoon pepper
1½ pounds stew beef, cut into 1-inch cubes
3 tablespoons vegetable oil
3 medium onions, peeled, thickly sliced (2½ cups)
½ teaspoon crumbled dried thyme
¾ cup beer or stout
½ teaspoon dry mustard

Combine flour, salt, and pepper. Dredge meat in flour mixture, shaking off excess.

Heat oil in heavy skillet. Add onions; cook over moderate heat until lightly browned. Remove with slotted spoon; reserve.

Brown meat in oil in 2 batches, stirring occasionally to ensure even browning. Return meat and reserved onions to pan. Add thyme, beer, and mustard. Cover; bring to boil. Reduce heat to low; cook 1½ to 2 hours or until meat is very tender.

Serve stew with mashed potatoes or boiled new potatoes tossed with parsley butter. Makes 4 servings.

roast leg of lamb with accompaniments

1 5-pound whole leg of lamb or sirloin half leg of lamb
4 tablespoons butter or margarine
1 teaspoon crumbled dried rosemary
1 clove garlic, minced
Freshly ground pepper
6 to 8 medium potatoes
1 pound carrots, peeled, trimmed
8 brown-skinned onions

Wipe lamb with damp cloth; place in roasting pan.

Melt butter. Add rosemary, garlic, and pepper to taste. Brush lamb well with butter mixture. Roast at 325°F 2 hours. Add potatoes and carrots to pan; brush well with butter mixture. Return to oven.

Do not peel or clean onions; just place on oven shelf next to roasting pan. Place small drip pan on shelf below. Roast 1 hour more or until lamb has reached an internal temperature of 180°F and vegetables are easily pierced with fork.

Carve lamb; place vegetables in serving bowl. Peel back brittle brown skins on onions. Remove cooked onion inside; serve with plenty of butter, salt, and pepper. Serve lamb with pan gravy or Mint Sauce. Makes 6 to 8 servings.

mint sauce
¼ cup water
2 tablespoons granulated sugar
1 tablespoon dried mint (¼ cup chopped fresh mint)
3 tablespoons distilled white vinegar

Combine water, sugar, and mint in small saucepan; bring to boil, stirring constantly. Remove from heat; cover. Cool completely. Thirty minutes before serving, add vinegar; stir well.

corned-beef hash

4 tablespoons butter or margarine
1 small onion, minced
1 16-ounce can corned beef (or 2 cups chopped leftover corned beef)
3 medium potatoes, peeled, diced
¾ cup water
2 tablespoons catsup
1 teaspoon Worcestershire sauce
¼ teaspoon garlic powder
Salt and pepper
4 eggs (optional)

Melt butter in large, heavy skillet. Add onion; sauté until tender. Add remaining ingredients, except eggs; stir well. Bring to boil over moderate heat. Reduce heat to low; cook, covered, 45 minutes, stirring occasionally. Make 4 wells in hash. Break eggs into wells. Cover; cook on low 10 to 12 minutes or until whites of eggs are set.

Serve hash garnished with parsley and sliced tomatoes with French dressing. Makes 4 servings.

creamed ham and potatoes

3 tablespoons butter or margarine
¼ cup finely chopped onion
4 cups peeled, diced potatoes
2 cups milk
2 cups diced cooked ham
1 tablespoon flour
1 tablespoon water
Salt and pepper
½ cup shredded sharp cheddar cheese
Chopped parsley

Melt butter in large, heavy saucepan over moderate heat. Sauté onion until tender. Add potatoes and milk; stir well. Bring to low boil over moderate heat. Reduce heat to low; cook 10 minutes. Add ham; simmer 10 minutes or until potatoes are tender.

Combine flour and water; stir into potato mixture. Cook until thickened. Season to taste with salt and pepper.

Spoon mixture into individual serving dishes; top with cheese and chopped parsley. Makes 4 servings.

pork chops with apple cream gravy

6 center-cut pork chops, cut ½ inch thick (about 1½ pounds)
5 tablespoons flour
Salt and pepper
3 tablespoons butter or margarine
½ cup slivered onion
1 cup light cream (or half-and-half)
½ cup apple cider
1 large apple, peeled, cored, sliced ¼ inch thick
¼ teaspoon ground mace

Wipe pork chops with damp cloth.

Combine 3 tablespoons flour with salt and pepper to taste on piece of waxed paper. Dredge chops with flour mixture.

Melt butter in heavy skillet. Sauté onion in butter until tender. Remove with slotted spoon; reserve.

Brown pork chops in remaining butter. Reserve.

Add 2 tablespoons flour to pan drippings; stir well. Cook 2 minutes or until bubbly but not brown. Reduce heat to low; gradually add cream, stirring constantly. Stir in apple cider and salt; cook until bubbly. Stir in onions. Arrange chops in gravy; top with apple slices. Sprinkle with mace; cover. Cook on low 15 minutes.

Serve chops hot with mashed potatoes. Makes 4 to 6 servings.

beer-braised pork roast

1 5-pound pork loin roast
2 tablespoons vegetable oil
2 medium onions, peeled, sliced

1 teaspoon salt
½ teaspoon pepper
1 12-ounce can or bottle Guiness stout or dark beer

Wipe meat with damp cloth.

Heat oil in Dutch oven over moderate heat. Brown meat on all sides. Remove to platter.

Add onions to pan; sauté until tender.

Place pork roast in Dutch oven; spoon onions over roast. Sprinkle with salt and pepper. Add beer. Cover; bring to boil over moderate heat. Reduce heat to low; cook approximately 2½ hours or until roast is fork-tender. Remove roast to warm platter; thicken pan juices if desired.

Slice roast. Serve with applesauce. Makes 5 servings.

pork ciste

pastry crust
1 cup flour
½ teaspoon salt

3 tablespoons lard
2 to 3 tablespoons cold water

pork and apple filling
1½ pounds lean pork, cut into 1-inch cubes
1 cup water
½ cup chopped onion
1 teaspoon crumbled dried sage leaves
¾ teaspoon salt
½ cup milk
¼ cup flour
2 large tart apples, peeled, cored, sliced
1 tablespoon sugar

1 egg yolk
1 tablespoon milk

First prepare pastry crust. Combine flour and salt, mixing well. Cut in lard until mixture resembles coarse meal. Add water a tablespoon at a time, while stirring with a fork, just until mixture holds together. Form into ball. Cover with plastic wrap; refrigerate.

Brown pork in large saucepan over moderate heat, stirring frequently. Add water, onion, sage, and salt; mix well. Cover; simmer over low heat 30 minutes or until meat is tender.

Combine milk and flour; stir to form smooth mixture. Add to pork mixture in saucepan, stirring constantly to prevent lumps from forming. Cook over low heat until thickened and bubbly. Pour ½ of pork mixture into 1½-quart lightly greased casserole. Top with apples; sprinkle with sugar. Add remaining pork mixture.

Roll pastry crust. Turn out dough onto lightly floured board; roll to fit casserole dish. Place over meat mixture. Turn under small margin of pastry around edge of casserole; crimp edge. Cut several steam vents in pastry.

Beat egg yolk and milk together; brush crust well with egg wash. Bake at 450°F 10 minutes. Reduce heat to 350°F; bake 25 minutes more. Serve hot. Makes 4 to 5 servings.

corned beef and
cabbage

1 3-pound corned-beef brisket
Cold water to cover
1 small onion, peeled, studded
   with 4 whole cloves

1 clove garlic, peeled, crushed
1 bay leaf
4 peppercorns
1 medium head cabbage

Wipe beef with damp cloth. Place in Dutch oven; cover with cold water. Add onion, garlic, bay leaf, and peppercorns. Bring to boil over moderate heat. Skim any foam; cover. Reduce heat to low; cook approximately 3 hours or until tender. Remove meat; keep warm.

Wash cabbage; cut into 4 wedges. Cut out core; remove any damaged outside leaves. Tie each wedge with kitchen string as you would a package.

Bring meat stock to boil. Add cabbage; cook 12 to 15 minutes or until cabbage is tender. Drain well; dress with butter, salt, and pepper.

Slice corned beef. Serve with cabbage and boiled potatoes. The following horseradish sauce is a spicy addition.

horseradish sauce
½ **cup sour cream**
½ **cup mayonnaise**
2 tablespoons (or more) prepared hot horseradish
1 tablespoon chopped parsley

Mix all ingredients together, adding horseradish to taste. Let stand at least 1 hour before serving.

corned beef and cabbage

shepherd's pie

This dish makes leftover roast a delicious treat!

1 cup peeled, sliced carrots
1 medium onion, peeled, sliced
3 cups diced cooked roast lamb or beef
½ cup frozen peas, slightly thawed
Salt and pepper
1 cup leftover gravy (or 1 cup canned gravy)
2 cups thick mashed potatoes
1 egg
2 tablespoons milk

Place carrots in small saucepan. Barely cover with water; cook until fork-tender. Drain.

Meanwhile, in separate saucepan cook onion, barely covered with water, until tender; drain.

Combine lamb, vegetables, and salt and pepper to taste in 2-quart casserole; mix well.

Heat gravy; thin with boiling water if it has become very thick. Pour gravy over meat and vegetables; stir to combine. Bake, uncovered, at 350°F 20 minutes.

Place potatoes in pastry bag and pipe over top of meat mixture, or mound over top of casserole with spoon.

Beat egg and milk together; brush potatoes with mixture. Return to oven; bake 20 minutes. Turn on broiler unit; cook until potatoes are lightly browned. Serve hot. Makes 4 servings.

shepherd's pie

hamburger steaks baked with cream

hamburger steaks baked with cream

1½ pounds lean ground beef
½ cup dry bread crumbs
3 tablespoons chopped onion
1 teaspoon Worcestershire sauce
1 egg
Salt and pepper
2 tablespoons butter or margarine
1 medium onion, peeled, chopped
2 carrots, peeled, chopped
2 stalks celery, chopped
1 tablespoon flour
1 cup light cream
1 10¾-ounce can cream of celery soup
2 tablespoons chopped parsley

Combine ground beef, bread crumbs, onion, Worcestershire sauce, egg, salt, and pepper in mixing bowl; mix well. Form into 8 patties.

Melt butter in heavy skillet over moderate heat. Fry meat patties until well-browned on both sides. Remove to 13 × 9 × 2-inch baking dish.

Add onion, carrots, and celery to pan drippings; sauté until tender. Add flour; stir until well-blended.

Combine cream and cream of celery soup. Add to vegetables. Reduce heat to low; cook until mixture is hot and well-blended. Pour over hamburgers in casserole. Cover tightly with aluminum foil. Bake at 350°F 1 hour.

Serve hamburgers with mashed potatoes, garnished with chopped parsley. Makes 4 servings.

29

irish stew

1½ pounds boneless lamb for stew
2 large onions, peeled, thickly sliced
5 medium potatoes, peeled, quartered, cut into chunks
2 stalks celery, sliced
1 turnip, diced
Salt and pepper
1½ cups chicken broth
1 bay leaf
Chopped parsley

Cut lamb into 1-inch cubes, removing large pieces of fat. Wipe meat with damp cloth or paper towels. Layer vegetables and meat in 2½-quart lightly greased casserole, beginning and ending with vegetables. Salt and pepper each layer lightly. Add chicken broth and bay leaf; cover tightly. Bake at 325°F 2 hours. Stir; sprinkle with parsley. Remove bay leaf before serving. Makes 4 servings.

irish stew

venison stew

3 pounds venison, cut into 1½-inch cubes

marinade
¾ cup red wine
2 tablespoons olive oil
1 medium onion, chopped
3 juniper berries, crushed
1 bay leaf
1 clove garlic, peeled, crushed
6 peppercorns

stew
¼ pound salt pork, diced
¼ cup chopped shallot (or onion)
½ cup chopped celery
½ cup chopped carrot
Flour
1 cup beef broth
1 teaspoon crumbled dried thyme
½ cup port wine
3 tablespoons currant jelly

Wipe venison with damp cloth; place in large casserole or glass dish.

Combine all marinade ingredients; pour over venison. Cover tightly; marinate in refrigerator 24 hours, stirring 3 or 4 times. Drain meat; reserve marinade.

Fry salt pork in Dutch oven until lightly browned. Remove with slotted spoon; reserve.

Add shallot, celery, and carrot to pan drippings; sauté until tender. Remove from pan; reserve.

Pat venison dry with paper towels; dredge lightly in flour. Brown in salt-pork fat, turning to ensure even browning. Add reserved vegetables, salt pork, beef broth, and thyme.

Strain marinade; add to pan. Stir well. Cover; bring to boil. Reduce heat to low; cook 2 to 2½ hours or until meat is tender. Stir in port wine and currant jelly; simmer 15 minutes.

Serve venison stew with boiled new potatoes. Makes 6 servings.

slumgullion

1½ pounds ground lamb or beef
1 large onion, peeled, finely chopped
3 large potatoes, peeled, cubed
4 carrots, peeled, chopped
Water to cover
Salt and pepper to taste
1 tablespoon Worcestershire sauce

Brown meat in large skillet over moderate heat. Add onion as meat begins to color. Stir occasionally; break up large chunks of meat with spoon. Drain off fat. Add remaining ingredients; mix well. Bring to boil. Reduce heat to low; cook 1 hour. Stir occasionally. Mixture should be thick when done; vegetables should be tender.

Serve slumgullion over mashed potatoes. Makes 4 to 5 servings.

dublin coddle

This dish is traditionally served on Saturday night with lots of bread and stout.

1 pound large pork-sausage links
4 to 6 thick slices bacon (approximately ½ pound), cut into
   2-inch pieces
¾ pound onions (3 medium)
1½ pounds potatoes (4 medium)
Black pepper
Finely chopped parsley

Prick sausages in several places. Place sausage and bacon in skillet; barely cover with water (about 3 cups). Bring to boil. Cover; simmer 10 minutes. Drain; reserve liquid.

Peel and slice onions.

Peel and thinly slice potatoes.

Layer sausage, bacon, onions, and potatoes in 2½-quart casserole. Lightly pepper layers. Pour broth from sausages into casserole to barely cover meat and vegetables (about 2½ cups). Cover casserole with waxed paper; bake at 350°F 1 hour or until potatoes are tender.

Sprinkle dish with parsley. Serve. Makes 4 to 5 servings.

roast cornish game hens with savory stuffing

4 Cornish game hens, approximately 1 pound each
8 thick slices home-style white bread
1½ tablespoons parsley flakes
¾ teaspoon salt
½ teaspoon poultry seasoning
¼ teaspoon freshly ground pepper
¾ cup butter
1 cup finely chopped onions
4 livers from Cornish hens
Salt and pepper
3 tablespoons melted butter

Remove giblet packs from hens; reserve livers. Wash Cornish hens; pat dry.

Cut crusts from bread; cut into ½-inch cubes. Place bread cubes on cookie sheet. Bake at 350°F until golden, stirring occasionally. Remove from oven; combine with parsley, ¾ teaspoon salt, poultry seasoning, and pepper; set aside.

Melt ¾ cup butter in heavy skillet. Add onions and livers; cook until livers are lightly browned and onions are tender. Remove livers; chop. Add livers, cooked onions, and butter from pan to bread cubes. Toss to mix well.

Salt and pepper hens lightly. Pack stuffing tightly into birds; truss. Place in ovenproof baking dish, breast-side-up; brush with melted butter. Roast at 375°F. Turn birds every 15 minutes; baste with any remaining butter and pan juices. Cook a total of 45 minutes to 1 hour or until juices run clear when tip of knife is inserted in bird.

Serve hens hot with wild rice and a green vegetable. Makes 4 servings.

32

chicken 'n cabbage

1 2½- to 3-pound chicken, cut up
Juice of ½ lemon
3 tablespoons butter
Salt and pepper
¾ cup white wine
3 tablespoons bacon fat
1 medium onion, finely chopped
3 cups shredded cabbage
1 cup diced celery
¼ cup diced green pepper
2 cups diced tomatoes
¼ teaspoon garlic powder
Salt and freshly ground pepper

Wash chicken; pat dry. Sprinkle with lemon juice.

Heat butter in heavy skillet until melted. Add chicken; cook over moderate heat until well-browned. Season with salt and pepper. Add wine; reduce heat to low. Cover; simmer 45 minutes or until chicken is tender.

Melt bacon fat in separate skillet over moderate heat. Add onion; cook 3 minutes, stirring constantly. Add cabbage, celery, green pepper, and tomatoes; mix well. Season with garlic powder, salt, and pepper. Cover. Reduce heat to low; cook 10 minutes. Vegetables should be crisp-tender.

Place cabbage in serving dish; top with chicken. Serve immediately. Makes 4 servings.

chicken with brandy cream

3 tablespoons butter, divided
1 tablespoon oil
1 cup slivered onion
½ pound mushrooms, cleaned, sliced
¼ cup flour
Salt and pepper
4 chicken breast fillets (1 pound total) *or* bone and skin 1½ pounds split chicken breasts
2 tablespoons brandy
1 cup heavy cream
½ teaspoon crumbled dried tarragon
1 egg yolk

Heat 2 tablespoons butter and the oil in heavy skillet over moderate heat. Add onion; sauté until tender. Add mushrooms; sauté 3 minutes, stirring occasionally. Remove from pan with slotted spoon; reserve.

Combine flour, salt, and pepper; dredge chicken breasts in mixture.

Add remaining 1 tablespoon butter to skillet; melt over moderate heat. Add chicken; brown well on both sides.

Warm brandy. Ignite; pour over chicken. Add cream and tarragon; heat through.

Beat egg yolk well. Add some of hot sauce to egg yolk; beat. Add to chicken; mix well. Add mushrooms and onions. Cook, stirring frequently, until thickened. Serve immediately. (Take care not to boil mixture after adding cream.) Makes 4 servings.

goose with potato stuffing

1 8- to 9-pound young goose, thawed if frozen

potato stuffing

3 medium potatoes (approximately 1 pound), peeled
1½ teaspoons salt
¼ pound lean salt pork, diced
¼ cup finely chopped onion
¼ pound bulk sausage
¼ cup butter or margarine
1 egg
½ teaspoon pepper
1 teaspoon crumbled sage leaves

Remove giblets from goose; wash well. Pat dry with paper towels. Salt lightly inside and out; set aside while making stuffing.

Place potatoes in medium saucepan. Cover with cold water; add ½ teaspoon salt. Bring to boil over moderate heat. Cover; cook on low 20 to 30 minutes or until tender. Drain. Place tea towel over pan; steam gently a few minutes.

Meanwhile, cook salt pork in heavy skillet over moderate heat until lightly browned. Remove with slotted spoon; reserve.

Add onion to skillet; cook until tender. Remove with slotted spoon; add to salt pork.

Add sausage to skillet; cook until lightly browned, breaking into small chunks as sausage cooks. Remove with slotted spoon; add to salt-pork mixture.

Put potatoes through ricer or mash with potato masher.

Combine salt-pork mixture, potatoes, and remaining stuffing ingredients; mix well. Allow to cool.

Stuff goose with potato mixture; truss bird. Place in open roasting pan, breast-side-up, on rack or trivet. Prick goose well on legs and wing joints to release fat. Roast in preheated 325°F oven 2 to 2½ hours or until leg joint moves easily. Allow to stand 15 to 20 minutes before carving.

Carve goose; remove dressing to serving dish. Serve with applesauce. Makes 6 servings.

goose with potato stuffing

chicken pie

1 2- to 2½-pound chicken
2 cups water
½ cup white wine
1 stalk celery, sliced
1 carrot, peeled, sliced
1 shallot, peeled, chopped
½ teaspoon salt
½ teaspoon poultry seasoning
4 slices crisp bacon, crumbled
2 hard-boiled eggs, peeled, quartered
1 medium onion, peeled, diced
2 tablespoons chopped parsley
1½ cups mushrooms, cleaned, quartered
3 tablespoons butter
3 tablespoons flour
2 cups reserved stock
Salt and pepper
3 tablespoons cream
2 frozen puff pastry shells (from 10-ounce package), defrosted
1 egg yolk

Wash chicken; pat dry. Place in large saucepan with water, wine, celery, carrot, shallot, ½ teaspoon salt, and poultry seasoning. Bring to boil; reduce heat to low. Cook 40 minutes or until cooked through. Strain; reserve stock. Cool chicken. Skin, bone, and cut chicken into 1-inch pieces.

Combine chicken, bacon, eggs, onion, parsley, and mushrooms in 9½-inch pie plate; set aside.

Melt butter in medium saucepan. Add flour; cook, stirring constantly, until bubbly. Add 2 cups stock, salt, and pepper; cook, stirring constantly, until thickened. Stir in 2 tablespoons cream; pour over chicken mixture.

Lightly flour pastry cloth. Stack puff pastry shells one on top of other; flatten with heels of your hands to 4-inch circle. Very carefully roll with floured rolling pin to 9½-inch circle; place on top of pie. Turn edge of crust under; do not attach to pie pan. Cut small circle from center of crust to serve as steam vent. Roll any scraps for decoration. Cut into leaf shapes; place on crust.

Beat together egg yolk and 1 tablespoon cream; brush crust well.

Preheat oven to 425°F; bake pie 10 minutes. Reduce heat to 375°F; cook 20 minutes. If crust begins to brown too quickly, cover lightly with foil. Serve hot. Makes 4 to 6 servings.

chicken pie

rabbit cooked in stout

rabbit cooked in stout

1 2½- to 3-pound rabbit, disjointed
½ cup flour
¼ teaspoon paprika
Salt and pepper
¼ pound salt pork, diced
1 pound pearl onions, cleaned, peeled
½ pound button mushrooms, cleaned, stems removed
1½ cups stout or dark beer
2 tablespoons chopped parsley
1 bay leaf
½ teaspoon crumbled dried thyme
2 tablespoons butter
2 tablespoons flour

Wash rabbit; pat dry.

Combine flour, paprika, salt, and pepper on piece of waxed paper. Dredge rabbit in flour mixture; shake off excess.

Cook salt pork in heavy skillet until lightly browned. Remove with slotted spoon; reserve.

Add rabbit to pan drippings; brown well on all sides. Place rabbit in large casserole. Add onions, mushrooms, and salt pork to casserole.

Combine stout, parsley, bay leaf, thyme, salt, and pepper; pour over rabbit. Cover; bake at 350°F 1½ hours.

Knead butter and flour together until well-blended.

Place rabbit in warm serving dish; keep warm while thickening sauce.

Place casserole on burner if it is stove-top safe, or transfer pan juices to small saucepan. Cook over low heat 2 to 3 minutes. Add butter and flour mixture in small balls to sauce, stirring well. Cook over low heat 5 minutes, stirring constantly. Pour over rabbit. Serve. Makes 4 to 5 servings.

vegetables

champ

4 large or 6 medium potatoes
Cold water
1 teaspoon salt
½ cup milk

½ cup sliced green onions
   or leeks
Salt and pepper
4 tablespoons melted butter

Peel potatoes; remove eyes. Quarter large potatoes; halve medium potatoes. Place in large saucepan. Cover with cold water; add salt. Bring to boil. Reduce heat to low; cook approximately 20 minutes or until tender. Drain well; return to saucepan. Place tea towel between pan and lid; steam over very low heat 10 minutes.

While potatoes are cooking, combine milk and onions in small saucepan; bring to gentle boil. Reduce heat; cook 2 minutes. Reserve.

Place hot potatoes in mixing bowl.

Strain onions from milk mixture. Reserve onions.

Beat potatoes with just enough hot milk to make stiff mashed potatoes. Fold in onions. Season with salt and pepper. Place in warm serving dish. Make well in center; pour in melted butter.

Serve champ immediately. Each diner serves himself some potatoes and butter. Makes 4 servings.

bubble and squeak

This dish is named for the noise it makes in the skillet as it cooks.

3 tablespoons butter or bacon fat
1 small onion, peeled, diced
2 cups shredded cooked cabbage
2 cups leftover mashed potatoes

Heat butter over moderate heat until melted. Add onion; sauté until tender.

Combine cabbage and mashed potatoes. Add to skillet; press with fork to form large cake. Cook over moderate heat until well-browned. Loosen potato cake with spatula; slide onto plate. Flip back into skillet, uncooked-side-down. Cook until well-browned. Serve this cut into wedges. Makes 4 servings.

pickled red cabbage

Delicious served with meat or poultry.

1 medium red cabbage (3 pounds)
⅓ cup coarse salt
1 quart malt vinegar
¼ cup sugar
2 tablespoons mixed pickling spices
2 bay leaves
½ teaspoon peppercorns

Core cabbage; discard any coarse leaves. Wash well; drain. Finely shred cabbage. Place in large stainless-steel or glass bowl. Add salt; stir well. Let stand in cool place 2 days, stirring well several times a day. On the third day drain cabbage well; squeeze dry in old towel. Place in canning jars.

Combine remaining ingredients in large saucepan. Bring to boil; cook, stirring, 5 minutes. Cool; strain. Pour over cabbage in jars. Cover; refrigerate. Allow to age 3 days before serving. Will keep 6 weeks in refrigerator. Makes 4 pints.

creamed cauliflower

1 10½-ounce package frozen cauliflower
Boiling salted water
1 cup milk
1½ tablespoons butter or margarine
1½ tablespoons flour
2 tablespoons water
Salt and pepper
½ teaspoon dry mustard
2 tablespoons chopped parsley

Cook cauliflower in boiling salted water to cover until fork-tender. Drain. Add milk and butter; heat over moderate heat 2 to 3 minutes.

Combine flour and water; mix well. Add to cauliflower; cook, stirring constantly, over low heat until thickened. Season with salt, pepper, and mustard.

Transfer cauliflower to heated serving dish; garnish with parsley. Serve. Makes 4 servings.

carrots cooked in milk

¾ pound baby carrots
1 tablespoon butter
⅔ cup milk
½ teaspoon sugar
¼ cup cream

2 egg yolks
Salt and pepper
Dash of mace
1 tablespoon chopped parsley

Trim carrots; scrub well with stiff brush. Split in half lengthwise any carrots longer than 2½ inches.

Melt butter in heavy saucepan. Add milk, sugar, and carrots; stir well. Cover; bring just to boil over medium heat. Reduce heat to low; cook approximately 10 minutes, until fork-tender.

Beat cream and egg yolks well. Stir slowly into carrot mixture. Cook over low heat, stirring frequently, until thickened. (Do *not* let mixture boil, as it will curdle.) Season to taste with salt and pepper; add dash of mace.

Place carrots in warm serving dish; top with chopped parsley. Makes 4 servings.

glazed carrots and onions

1 pound carrots, peeled, sliced
   ½ inch thick
1½ cups peeled, sliced white
   onions
Water
1 teaspoon salt

3 tablespoons butter
1 tablespoon brown sugar
1½ tablespoons lemon juice
2 teaspoons cornstarch
3 tablespoons water

Combine carrots and onions in medium saucepan. Add enough cold water just to cover vegetables; add salt. Cover saucepan; bring to boil. Reduce heat to low; cook 10 to 12 minutes or until crisp-tender. Drain well; keep warm.

Melt butter in small saucepan over low heat. Add brown sugar; stir to dissolve. Add lemon juice; stir well.

Combine cornstarch and 3 tablespoons water. Add to sugar mixture; stir to combine. Cook over low heat, stirring constantly, until thickened.

Combine carrots, onions, and sauce; stir well.

Serve this immediately in warm serving dish. Makes 4 to 6 servings.

old-fashioned salad

1 small head lettuce
1 hard-boiled egg

salad dressing
2 hard-boiled eggs, very
   finely chopped
2 teaspoons malt vinegar
2 teaspoons dry mustard

1 large tomato, cut in wedges
¼ cup finely sliced onion

2 teaspoons sugar
½ cup sour cream
½ cup mayonnaise
Salt and pepper

Clean lettuce; tear into bite-size pieces. Dry with paper towel.

Peel and slice hard-boiled egg; arrange with tomato and onion on lettuce in salad bowl. Refrigerate until serving time.

Thoroughly mix hard-boiled eggs, vinegar, mustard, and sugar. Add sour cream, mayonnaise, and salt and pepper to taste; mix well. Refrigerate 1 hour before serving.

Pour dressing over prepared salad. Serve. Makes 4 servings.

parsley-buttered new potatoes

8 to 12 small new potatoes (number depends on size)
2 cups water
1½ teaspoons salt
¼ cup melted butter
2 tablespoons finely chopped parsley
Salt and pepper

Scrub potatoes well.

Bring water and 1½ teaspoons salt to boil in large saucepan over high heat. Add potatoes; cover. Bring to boil; reduce heat to low. Cook 10 to 15 minutes or until just tender. Drain; place folded tea towel over pan. Place cover on pan; return to burner. Allow to steam on very low heat a few minutes (the residual heat in an electric burner is sufficient). Remove towel. Add butter, parsley, and salt and pepper to taste. Serve immediately. Makes 4 servings.

turnip bake

1 pound rutabagas
½ pound white turnips
4 slices bacon, diced
¼ cup chopped onion
1 cup water
Salt and pepper
Chopped parsley

Peel rutabagas and turnips; cut into small cubes.

Cook bacon in heavy skillet until crisp; remove from pan. Crumble; reserve.

Add onion to bacon fat in skillet; cook until tender. Add water, salt, and pepper; bring to boil.

Combine rutabagas, turnips, and reserved bacon in 2-quart casserole. Add boiling water and onion. Cover; bake at 350°F 45 minutes or until fork-tender.

Sprinkle casserole with chopped parsley. Serve. Makes 6 servings.

summer mixed vegetables

2 medium carrots, peeled, sliced
1 medium turnip, peeled, diced into ½-inch cubes
1 cup frozen peas
2 tablespoons butter or margarine
½ teaspoon sugar
1 tablespoon water
Salt and pepper

Cook each vegetable in separate, small saucepan in boiling salted water until crisp-tender. Drain well.

Melt butter in medium saucepan. Add sugar, water, salt, and pepper; mix well. Add vegetables; cook, stirring, 3 minutes, until glazed and water has evaporated. Serve immediately. Makes 4 servings.

41

dunmurry rice

2 tablespoons butter
1 small onion, finely minced
1 cup converted rice
1 cup sliced mushrooms
2½ cups chicken stock or broth
2 tablespoons chopped parsley
Salt and pepper
3 medium tomatoes
2 tablespoons butter or margarine, melted
½ cup fine dry bread crumbs
1 tablespoon grated Parmesan cheese
Paprika

Melt butter in heavy saucepan. Add onion, rice, and mushrooms; sauté until rice starts to brown. Add stock, parsley, salt, and pepper; bring to boil. Reduce heat to low; cook, covered, 25 minutes or until all liquid is absorbed.

Grease 1-quart mixing bowl. Pack rice into bowl tightly. Keep warm while preparing tomatoes.

Split tomatoes in half.

Combine melted butter, bread crumbs, cheese, salt, pepper, and paprika; mix well. Sprinkle crumb mixture over tomatoes; broil in preheated broiler 4 inches from heat until golden.

Unmold rice onto warm serving dish; surround with tomatoes. Serve. Makes 6 servings.

colcannon

This dish is traditionally served on Halloween night.

4 large or 6 medium potatoes
Cold water
1 teaspoon salt
4 cups finely shredded cabbage
2 cups boiling salted water
½ cup warm milk
Salt and pepper
4 tablespoons butter, melted

Peel potatoes; remove eyes. Cut large potatoes in quarters; cut medium potatoes in half. Place in large saucepan; cover with cold water. Add salt; bring to boil. Reduce heat to low; cook approximately 20 minutes or until fork-tender. Drain well; return to saucepan. Place tea towel between pan and lid; steam over very low heat 10 minutes.

Meanwhile, cook cabbage in boiling salted water 5 minutes. Drain well; reserve.

Mash potatoes with warm milk. Season with salt and pepper. Beat in cooked cabbage to form pale-green fluff. Place in warm serving dish. Make well in center; pour in melted butter. Serve immediately. Makes 4 to 5 servings.

variation
An equal amount of shredded kale may be substituted for cabbage in this recipe.

cabbage with bacon

cabbage with bacon

1 medium head cabbage (about 2 pounds)
1 quart meat stock (preferably water in which ham, corned beef, or
    sausage was cooked)
4 slices crisply fried bacon, crumbled
2 tablespoons melted butter
Salt
Freshly ground black pepper
Ground mace

Quarter cabbage head. Remove any coarse outside leaves; cut out core. Tie with kitchen cord as you would a package.

Bring stock to boil in large saucepan. Add cabbage wedges; cook, covered, over low heat 15 to 20 minutes or until tender. Remove from saucepan, draining well.

Place cabbage in warm serving dish. Drizzle with melted butter; sprinkle lightly with salt, pepper, and mace. Garnish with crumbled bacon. Serve. Makes 4 to 6 servings.

irish minted peas

1 10-ounce package frozen green peas
1 teaspoon dried mint
1 teaspoon sugar
Boiling salted water
1 tablespoon butter or margarine
Salt and pepper to taste

Cook peas, mint, and sugar in boiling salted water to cover 5 to 7 minutes or until peas are tender. Drain; stir in butter, salt, and pepper. Serve immediately. Makes 4 servings.

creamed peas and potatoes

Delicious served with fish dishes.

3 medium potatoes, peeled, diced
Cold water
1 teaspoon salt
1 10-ounce package frozen green peas
2 cups milk
2 tablespoons butter or margarine
1 tablespoon flour
1 tablespoon water
Salt and pepper

Place potatoes in medium saucepan. Add cold water to barely cover potatoes; add 1 teaspoon salt. Bring to boil over moderate heat; cook 10 to 15 minutes or until tender. Drain.

Meanwhile, cook peas according to package directions. Drain; keep warm until needed.

Add milk and butter to potatoes; heat until bubbling.

Combine flour and 1 tablespoon water; mix well. Add to potatoes; cook, stirring, until thickened. Add peas; mix well. Season with salt and pepper to taste. Makes 4 servings.

fresh potato cakes

4 medium potatoes
1 small onion
2 medium eggs, lightly beaten

1 tablespoon flour
1 teaspoon salt
½ cup vegetable oil

Peel potatoes and onion; grate both into mixing bowl. Add eggs, flour, and salt; mix well.

Heat oil in heavy skillet. Drop potato mixture into hot oil by ⅓ cupfuls, forming ragged cakes. Cook over moderate heat until crisp and brown, turning once. Drain on absorbent paper. Serve hot. Makes 4 servings (8 potato cakes).

fresh potato cakes

oakhill potatoes

oakhill potatoes

Delicious served with broiled lamb chops and green peas.

1½ pounds (4 to 5 medium) potatoes, peeled, diced
½ teaspoon salt
3 tablespoons butter or margarine
2 tablespoons flour
Salt and pepper
2 cups milk
2 hard-boiled eggs, peeled, sliced
2 tablespoons chopped onion
3 tablespoons dry bread crumbs

Place potatoes in large saucepan. Cover with cold water; add ½ teaspoon salt. Bring to boil. Reduce heat to low; cook 20 to 25 minutes or until potatoes are tender. Drain; reserve.

Melt 2 tablespoons butter in medium saucepan. Add flour, salt, and pepper; cook until bubbly. Add milk; stir well. Cook, stirring constantly, until thickened.

Combine potatoes, hard-boiled eggs, onion, salt, and pepper in lightly greased 1½-quart casserole. Add white sauce; blend lightly with spatula.

Melt remaining 1 tablespoon butter. Add bread crumbs; mix well. Sprinkle buttered crumbs over casserole. Bake at 350°F 30 minutes. Serve. Makes 4 servings.

potato collops

¼ pound bacon, diced
1½ pounds potatoes, peeled, sliced
1½ tablespoons flour
3 tablespoons chopped onion
1½ teaspoons parsley flakes
Salt and pepper
1½ cups hot milk

Place bacon in heavy skillet; fry 4 to 5 minutes or until lightly browned but not crisp.

Grease 1½-quart casserole. Place ¼ of potatoes in bottom. Sprinkle with ½ tablespoon flour, 1 tablespoon onion, ½ teaspoon parsley flakes, ⅓ of cooked bacon, and 1 teaspoon bacon fat. Sprinkle lightly with salt and pepper. Top with ¼ of potatoes. Continue layering until all ingredients are used, ending with potatoes. Pour milk down side of casserole. Cover; bake 30 minutes at 350°F. Uncover; cook 60 minutes. Serve hot. Makes 4 servings.

luncheon salad

1 cup water
Salt
1 10-ounce package frozen green beans
1 pound small new potatoes, peeled
Boiling water
½ teaspoon salt
½ pound boiled ham, cut into strips
4 tomatoes, quartered
10 pimiento-stuffed olives, sliced

salad dressing
6 tablespoons olive oil
3 tablespoons malt vinegar
½ teaspoon garlic salt
1 teaspoon sugar
½ teaspoon pepper

1 head Boston lettuce

Bring 1 cup water and salt to boil in medium saucepan. Add green beans; cook, covered, over low heat 7 to 10 minutes. Drain.

Meanwhile, place potatoes in large saucepan; barely cover with boiling water. Add ½ teaspoon salt; bring to boil. Cover; cook 15 to 20 minutes or until tender. Drain. Steam in pot a few minutes; cool. Slice.

Combine green beans, sliced potatoes, ham, tomatoes, and olives in large salad bowl; mix gently.

Combine all salad dressing ingredients in container of electric blender; blend 1 minute. Pour dressing over salad; mix. Refrigerate several hours before serving.

Line individual serving bowls with Boston lettuce; add salad. Serve. Makes 3 to 4 servings.

luncheon salad

pickled beets

2 bunches beets
Boiling salted water
1 medium onion, peeled, sliced, separated into rings
½ cup vinegar
½ cup water
2 tablespoons sugar
⅛ teaspoon ground cloves
½ teaspoon salt
3 peppercorns
½ bay leaf

Wash beets well. Leave root ends intact; cut off all but 2 inches of tops. Cook in boiling salted water until fork-tender. Cooking time will depend on size of beets, but allow at least 15 minutes. Alternately, beets may be wrapped in foil and baked in 375°F oven until tender (45 minutes to 1 hour). Cool beets 15 minutes; peel. Slice or quarter beets. Place beets and onion rings in canning jar.
Combine remaining ingredients in small saucepan; bring to boil. Remove from heat; pour over beets. Cover; refrigerate several days before use. Makes 2½ to 3 cups.

Note: Liquid from pickled beets can be reserved and used to pickle hard-cooked eggs, a favorite of beer-drinkers!

brussels sprouts au gratin

1 10-ounce package frozen brussels sprouts
Boiling salted water
2½ tablespoons butter or margarine
1½ tablespoons flour
Salt and pepper
1 cup milk
¾ cup grated sharp cheddar cheese
2 tablespoons bread crumbs
Parsley flakes
Paprika

Cook brussels sprouts in boiling salted water to cover until tender. Drain; reserve.

Melt 1½ tablespoons butter in medium saucepan. Add flour, salt, and pepper; cook until bubbly. Add milk; cook, stirring constantly, until thickened. Add cheese; stir well.

Place brussels sprouts in 1-quart lightly greased casserole. Top with sauce.

Melt 1 tablespoon butter. Add bread crumbs; mix well. Sprinkle over casserole. Sprinkle with parsley flakes; dust with paprika. Bake at 350°F 20 minutes. Serve. Makes 3 to 4 servings.

breads, cakes, and desserts

irish brown bread

1 cup unsifted all-purpose flour
2 tablespoons sugar
1 teaspoon baking powder
1 teaspoon baking soda
½ teaspoon salt
1½ tablespoons butter or margarine
2 cups whole-wheat flour (stone-ground if possible)
¼ cup rolled oats
1½ cups buttermilk

Combine all-purpose flour, sugar, baking powder, soda, and salt. Cut in butter until in very small particles. Stir in whole-wheat flour and rolled oats well. Make well in center; add buttermilk. Stir lightly but thoroughly until all flour is moistened. Turn out onto lightly floured board; knead 5 times. Gather into ball; place on lightly greased cookie sheet. Pat into 7-inch circle. Using sharp knife, make large cross on top of loaf to allow for expansion. Bake at 375°F 40 minutes, until loaf is browned and sounds hollow when tapped. Remove from oven; place on rack. Brush with melted butter. Allow to cool before serving. Makes 1 loaf, 7 inches in diameter.

variation
yellow-meal bread: Use 1½ cups all-purpose flour and 1½ cups finely ground cornmeal in place of flour and whole-wheat flour in recipe. Omit rolled oats. Mix as listed in above recipe.

oatmeal bread

2 cups boiling water
1 cup dry rolled oatmeal
2 packages active dry yeast
⅓ cup warm water (105 to 115°F)
2 teaspoons salt
½ cup honey
2 tablespoons melted butter
4 to 5 cups unsifted all-purpose flour
1 egg yolk
1 teaspoon water

Combine boiling water and oatmeal; let stand 30 minutes (oatmeal should be quite soft).

Combine yeast and warm water; stir until dissolved. Set aside.

Stir salt, honey, and butter into oatmeal, mixing well. Add yeast mixture; stir well. Gradually add enough flour to make dough that is not sticky and can be easily kneaded. Knead on lightly floured board 5 to 10 minutes, adding more flour as necessary, to form smooth, elastic dough. Place in oiled bowl, rotating to grease surface of dough. Cover; allow to rise in warm place, without drafts, until double in bulk (approximately 1½ hours).

Punch down dough; form into 2 loaves. Place in 2 greased 9 × 5-inch loaf pans. Cover; allow to rise until double in bulk (approximately 45 minutes).

Preheat oven to 350°F.

Meanwhile, beat egg yolk and water together. Brush loaves with mixture. Bake 50 to 60 minutes or until loaves are brown and sound hollow when tapped. Makes 2 9 × 5-inch loaves.

nora's best soda bread

4 cups unsifted all-purpose flour
2 tablespoons sugar
1 teaspoon baking soda
1 teaspoon salt
1 cup seedless raisins
1 to 1¼ cups buttermilk
2 tablespoons soft butter

Combine flour, sugar, soda, salt, and raisins in mixing bowl; stir well. Make well in center of mixture. Add buttermilk; stir until lightly but thoroughly blended. Use only enough buttermilk to make stiff dough. Turn out onto lightly floured board; knead 5 times. Form into ball; place on lightly greased cookie sheet. Pat to 8-inch circle, approximately 1½ inches thick. With floured knife make large cross on top of loaf to keep it from cracking during baking. Spread top of loaf with softened butter. Bake in preheated 375°F oven 40 to 50 minutes or until golden and loaf sounds hollow when tapped.

Serve bread hot, with plenty of butter. Makes 1 loaf, 8 inches in diameter.

boxty

1 cup peeled grated potato
1 cup cold mashed potatoes
2 cups all-purpose flour
2 tablespoons melted butter
¾ teaspoon salt
Pepper

Squeeze grated potato dry in tea towel. Combine grated potato in mixing bowl with mashed potatoes. Add flour, butter, salt, and pepper; mix well. Turn out onto floured board; knead 1 minute. Roll out to ½-inch-thick circle; cut into wedges. Bake on ungreased griddle over gentle heat 30 to 40 minutes; turn once. Bread should be well-browned.

Serve bread split and buttered. Makes 4 servings.

currant buns

1 13¾-ounce package hot-roll mix
¾ cup warm water
2 tablespoons soft butter
2 tablespoons currants
2 tablespoons seedless raisins
1 egg, lightly beaten
⅓ cup sugar
1 teaspoon ground cinnamon
½ teaspoon nutmeg
1 egg yolk
1 tablespoon milk

In large mixing bowl dissolve yeast from hot-roll mix in warm water. Add butter, currants, and raisins; mix well. Add egg; stir to combine. Add flour mixture from hot-roll mix, sugar, and spices; stir well to incorporate flour. Cover with towel; let stand in warm place 45 minutes or until double in bulk.

Punch down dough. Flour smooth surface; turn out dough. Knead until no longer sticky. Divide into 12 buns of equal size. Place in greased 9 × 9-inch-square pan. Cover with towel; let rise in warm place until double in bulk.

Beat together egg yolk and milk. Brush buns with mixture.

Preheat oven to 375°F; bake buns 15 minutes. Cool; ice with Confectioners' Sugar Icing. Makes 12 buns.

confectioners' sugar icing
1 cup sifted confectioners' sugar
½ teaspoon vanilla
Dash of salt
2 tablespoons milk

Combine sugar, vanilla, and salt. Add enough milk to make firm icing; drizzle over buns.

barmbrack

A golden ring is kneaded into the dough, and the lucky recipient is said to be married within the year.

4 cups all-purpose flour
¾ cup sugar
½ teaspoon ground cinnamon
¼ teaspoon ground allspice
⅛ teaspoon ground nutmeg
½ teaspoon salt
1 package active dry yeast
1 cup milk
3 tablespoons butter or margarine
1 egg, lightly beaten
1¼ cups golden raisins
½ cup currants
½ cup mixed chopped candied peel
1 tablespoon confectioners' sugar
2 tablespoons boiling water

Combine 1½ cups flour, sugar, spices, salt, and yeast; mix well.

Combine milk and butter in small saucepan; heat on low until very warm. Gradually add to dry ingredients; beat 2 minutes. Add egg and ½ cup flour; beat 2 minutes. Stir in enough of remaining flour to form stiff, elastic dough. Turn out onto lightly floured board; knead until smooth. Knead in fruit and peel. Place in greased bowl; cover. Set in warm place to rise until double in bulk (approximately 1½ hours).

Punch down dough; form into loaf or round ball. Place in greased 8-inch-round cake pan or casserole or greased 9 × 5 × 3-inch loaf pan. Cover; let rise until double in bulk (45 minutes).

Bake in preheated 400°F oven 50 to 60 minutes. Loaf should be well-browned and sound hollow when tapped.

Combine sugar and water; brush hot loaf. Return to oven 3 minutes. Remove loaf from pan; cool on wire rack. Makes 1 loaf (1 8-inch-round loaf or 1 9 × 5 × 3-inch loaf).

barmbrack

tea scones

2 cups all-purpose flour
1 tablespoon baking powder
½ teaspoon salt
1 tablespoon sugar
4 tablespoons butter or margarine
2 medium eggs
⅓ cup milk
1 egg, lightly beaten
1 tablespoon milk

Combine flour, baking powder, salt, and sugar in mixing bowl; mix well. Cut in butter. Make well in flour mixture.

Beat 2 eggs and ⅓ cup milk together. Add to flour mixture; mix lightly but thoroughly. Turn out onto floured board; knead 5 times. Roll dough to 9-inch circle approximately ¾ inch thick. Cut into 8 pie-shaped wedges. Place on lightly greased baking sheet.

Beat remaining egg and tablespoon of milk together. Brush tops of scones with mixture. Bake in preheated 400°F oven 7 to 10 minutes or until lightly browned.

Split scones. Serve with butter and jam or honey. Makes 8 scones.

variations
orange scones: Add 1 tablespoon grated orange rind to dry ingredients in basic recipe.
currant scones: Add ½ cup currants to dry ingredients in basic recipe.
oatmeal scones: Use 1 cup rolled oats and 1¼ cups flour in place of 2 cups flour in basic recipe.

tea scones

jam cake

This makes a delicious tea cake!

1¾ cups sifted cake flour
¾ teaspoon baking powder
⅛ teaspoon salt
4 eggs (room temperature)
¾ cup granulated sugar
1 teaspoon grated lemon rind
½ teaspoon lemon extract
1 cup strawberry, raspberry, or blueberry jam
Confectioners' sugar

Preheat oven to 350°F.

Sift together flour, baking powder, and salt; set aside.

Grease and flour 2 8-inch cake pans; line with waxed paper.

In large mixing bowl beat eggs until thick and lemon-colored. Gradually beat in sugar; mixture should be thick and light. Using spatula, fold in flour mixture, lemon rind, and lemon extract. Spread in prepared cake pans. Bake 20 to 25 minutes or until toothpick inserted in center comes out clean. Cool slightly. Turn out onto rack; remove paper immediately. Cool completely.

Center one layer on serving plate. Spread with jam; top with second layer. Top with sifted confectioners' sugar. Makes 6 servings.

jam cake

simnel cake

This cake was traditionally prepared on the third Sunday of Lent (Mothering Sunday) but was not served until Easter. It is a rich, moist cake with excellent keeping qualities.

1 cup butter	1 teaspoon ground ginger
1 cup sugar	½ teaspoon ground allspice
4 eggs	2 cups light (golden) raisins
2 tablespoons whiskey	1 cup dark seedless raisins
2 cups flour	1 cup currants
1 teaspoon baking powder	½ cup finely chopped citron
½ teaspoon salt	

marzipan mixture
2 7-ounce cans almond paste
2 cups confectioners' sugar
6 tablespoons light corn syrup

1 egg white, lightly beaten

Place several thicknesses of greased waxed paper in bottom of 9-inch springform pan; set aside.

Cream butter until light. Add sugar; continue creaming until well-mixed.

Beat together eggs and whiskey; add to butter and sugar, beating well.

Sift together flour, baking powder, salt, and spices.

Wash raisins and currants in hot water; pat dry with paper towel. Combine with chopped citron.

Add ½ of flour mixture to creamed mixture; stir well. Add fruits and remaining flour; mix thoroughly.

Next, prepare the Marzipan Mixture. In mixing bowl break almond paste into small pieces. Add confectioners' sugar and corn syrup; mix well. Divide into 3 equal parts.

Place ½ of cake batter in prepared pan.

On board dusted with confectioners' sugar roll ⅓ of marzipan to 9-inch circle. Place in cake pan on top of batter. Cover with remaining batter; spread evenly on top of marzipan. Bake cake in preheated 325°F oven 90 minutes. Turn oven off; let cake stand undisturbed in oven 30 minutes. Remove from oven. Cool; remove from pan.

Roll ⅓ of marzipan to 9-inch circle on confectioners'-sugar-dusted board.

Place cake on cookie sheet; brush top with beaten egg white. Place marzipan on top of cake; press down firmly so it adheres to cake.

Make 12 small balls with remaining marzipan. Place 1 ball in center of cake and others around edge in a circle.

Preheat broiler; lightly brown marzipan 3 to 4 inches from heat. Watch carefully.

This cake freezes well or can be kept in an airtight cake tin. Makes 10 to 12 servings.

ginger cake

1 cup firmly packed brown sugar
½ cup butter or margarine
¼ cup unsulfured molasses
2 cups all-purpose flour
2 teaspoons ground ginger
1½ teaspoons baking powder
½ teaspoon baking soda
⅛ teaspoon salt
1 egg, lightly beaten
½ cup milk, warmed

lemon butter icing
3 tablespoons soft butter or margarine
1½ cups confectioners' sugar, sifted
1 tablespoon lemon juice (approximately)

Combine brown sugar, butter, and molasses in small saucepan; cook over low heat until sugar is dissolved. Cool.

Grease and flour 8-inch-square cake pan; set aside.

Sift together flour, ginger, baking powder, soda, and salt into mixing bowl. Make well in center. Add cooled sugar mixture; mix well. Add egg and milk; continue beating 3 minutes. Pour mixture into prepared cake pan. Bake in preheated 325°F oven 45 minutes or until toothpick inserted in center of cake comes out clean. Let cake stand 5 minutes. Loosen from pan; turn out onto wire rack to cool completely. Place cake on serving dish.

Beat together soft butter, sugar, and enough lemon juice to make spreadable icing. Spread on sides and top of cake. Makes 6 servings.

shrove tuesday pancakes

These pancakes were traditionally served on Shrove Tuesday at tea time. All eggs and milk, which were forbidden during Lent, were used before Ash Wednesday.

2 cups sifted all-purpose flour
2 teaspoons baking soda
2 teaspoons sugar
½ teaspoon salt
2 eggs, lightly beaten
3 tablespoons melted butter or margarine
2 cups buttermilk

Sift dry ingredients together into mixing bowl.

Beat eggs, butter, and buttermilk together well. Add to dry ingredients; combine thoroughly without overmixing (small lumps may remain). Bake on a hot, lightly greased griddle or heavy frying pan until golden. Turn; continue cooking.

Serve pancakes hot, spread with butter and sprinkled with sugar. Makes 12 pancakes.

oatmeal porridge

Traditionally, oatmeal porridge is served with buttermilk. We like it with milk, butter, and brown sugar, or try a tablespoon of treacle syrup.

2 cups water
2 cups milk
1 teaspoon salt
1 cup Irish oatmeal
½ cup seedless raisins (optional)

Combine water, milk, and salt in heavy saucepan; bring to boil. Add oatmeal and raisins; cook, stirring constantly, until mixture is smooth and starting to thicken. Reduce heat to simmer; cook 30 minutes, stirring frequently. Makes 4 servings.

carrageen milk pudding

Carrageen is an edible form of dry seaweed, rich in vitamins, and noted for its gelling properties. It is available dry in health food or import stores.

½ cup tightly packed carrageen (½ ounce)
Boiling water
2 cups milk
¼ cup sugar
1 teaspoon vanilla extract
Food coloring (optional)

Pick over carrageen, discarding any foreign matter. Place in small bowl. Add boiling water to cover; stir. Drain.

Combine carrageen and milk in small saucepan; cook over moderate heat, stirring frequently, approximately 15 minutes or until mixture is thick and creamy. Add sugar and vanilla; stir until sugar is dissolved. Add food coloring, if desired. Strain mixture to remove carrageen; pour into individual molds, rinsed in cold water. Refrigerate several hours, until set. Unmold; serve with whipped cream or chocolate sauce. Makes 4 servings.

variations

lemon milk pudding: Add grated rind of 1 lemon to milk before cooking. Omit vanilla extract; substitute ½ teaspoon lemon extract. Tint with few drops yellow food coloring, if desired.

peppermint milk pudding: Omit vanilla extract; substitute ¼ teaspoon peppermint extract and few drops of green food coloring.

chocolate milk pudding: Combine 1 tablespoon unsweetened cocoa with sugar; add to milk mixture.

plum pudding

A traditional Christmas treat!

½ cup golden raisins
½ cup chopped citron
½ cup currants
½ cup seedless raisins
¾ cup Irish whiskey
1 cup brown sugar
½ cup chopped beef suet or butter
2 eggs
1½ cups bread crumbs
½ cup flour
½ teaspoon baking soda
¼ teaspoon salt
½ teaspoon ground allspice
¼ teaspoon ground nutmeg
½ teaspoon ground ginger
1¼ cups milk
1 teaspoon grated orange rind
1 teaspoon grated lemon rind
½ cup chopped almonds
Boiling water
3 tablespoons Irish whiskey

Combine dried fruits in small bowl. Add whiskey; mix well. Allow to stand 12 hours, stirring occasionally.

Cream sugar and suet until soft. Add eggs; mix well.

Combine bread crumbs, flour, soda, salt, and spices; add alternately with milk, mixing well after each addition. Add grated peels, soaked fruits, and nuts; stir well. Place in well-greased mold. Place mold on trivet in deep kettle. Cover top of mold with lid or 2 layers of cheesecloth tied to cover mold, topped with aluminum foil. Add boiling water ⅔ up side of mold; bring rapidly to boil. Reduce heat to low; boil 5 hours, adding more water as necessary. Cool; re-cover. Store in refrigerator until ready to serve.

Steam for an hour before serving to heat through. Unmold.

To serve, warm 3 tablespoons whiskey; ignite. Pour over pudding. Garnish with sprig of holly; serve immediately. Serve with Hard Sauce. Makes 12 servings.

hard sauce

Hard sauce is best prepared several days in advance and refrigerated until needed.

½ cup butter
1 cup powdered sugar
⅛ teaspoon salt
1 teaspoon vanilla extract
2 tablespoons cream
2 tablespoons Irish whiskey

Cream butter until light. Beat in sugar, salt, vanilla, and cream, mixing well. Refrigerate until needed. Just before serving, beat in whiskey.

stuffed baked apples

4 baking apples (for example, Rome Beauties or Greening apples)
½ cup prepared mincemeat
1 cup apple cider
2 tablespoons butter or margarine

Wash and core apples. Pare upper half of each apple to prevent splitting. Place apples upright in small baking dish. Fill cavities in apples with mincemeat. Pour apple cider around apples; dot tops of apples with butter. Bake at 375°F 30 to 40 minutes, basting with pan juices several times during cooking. Makes 4 servings.

tipsy parson

This dessert was named for its expected effect on the parson at tea time.

1 cup blackberries, raspberries, or strawberries, thawed if frozen
6 tablespoons sugar
½ stale sponge cake, cut into 1-inch cubes (4 to 5 cups cake cubes)
3 tablespoons sweet sherry
1 tablespoon cornstarch
¼ teaspoon salt
2 cups milk
2 eggs, slightly beaten
1 teaspoon vanilla extract
½ cup whipping cream, whipped
Additional whipped cream for garnish
Toasted almonds

If you have a decorative cut-glass or crystal bowl, it is the ideal container for this dessert. If not, assemble dessert in individual sherbet glasses.

Pick over fruit; wash well, cutting away stems and defects. Drain well. Combine fruit and 2 tablespoons sugar in bowl; set aside.

Toss cake cubes and sherry in separate bowl; set aside.

Combine 4 tablespoons sugar, cornstarch, and salt in heavy saucepan; stir to combine. Add milk; stir until well-blended. Cook over moderate heat, stirring constantly, until mixture boils. Add small amount of hot mixture to beaten eggs; beat well. Slowly add egg mixture to saucepan, stirring constantly. Reduce heat to low; cook, stirring constantly, until mixture begins to bubble. Stir in vanilla; cool 15 minutes. Fold in whipped cream.

Layer cake squares, fruit, and custard in serving bowl or individual dishes. Refrigerate at least 4 hours before serving. Decorate with whipped cream and toasted almonds. Makes 6 servings.

Note: Any fruit can be substituted for berries. Drain canned fruit; sweeten fresh fruits to taste.

madigan's velvet trousers

This recipe comes from a friend of my mother's who grew up in Ireland. The fanciful name is almost as much fun as eating this delicious dessert!

1 package (¼ ounce) unflavored gelatin
¼ cup cold water
½ cup heavy cream
½ cup light cream
1½ tablespoons clear honey
2 tablespoons Irish whiskey

Soak gelatin in cold water in small measuring cup. Set measuring cup in saucepan of gently boiling water; stir until gelatin dissolves (approximately 3 minutes). Remove from pan of water; set aside.

Combine creams in small well-chilled bowl; whip until light and thick. Slowly add honey and whiskey, mixing well. Place bowl in pan of ice water; fold in dissolved gelatin. Continue to mix and gently fold mixture until it begins to set. Spoon into 4 small glass serving dishes; cover. Refrigerate several hours before serving.

Serve this with lady fingers or small fancy cookies. Makes 4 servings.

irish coffee mold

1¼ cups coffee
¼ cup sugar
2 cloves
1 strip lemon peel
1 strip orange peel
1 small piece cinnamon stick
1 envelope unflavored gelatin
¼ cup Irish Mist or whiskey
Lightly whipped cream, flavored with sugar and vanilla extract

Combine coffee, sugar, cloves, lemon peel, orange peel, and cinnamon in small saucepan. Bring to boil; boil 2 minutes. Strain.

Soften gelatin in Irish Mist. Add hot-coffee mixture to gelatin; stir until gelatin is dissolved.

Rinse 3 or 4 small molds with cold water. Pour in gelatin mixture; chill overnight.

Unmold at serving time by dipping molds briefly in hot water. Top with whipped cream. Makes 3 to 4 servings.

chocolate potato cake

chocolate potato cake

1 medium potato
1½ ounces semisweet chocolate
⅔ cup butter
6 tablespoons sugar
2 eggs
1 teaspoon vanilla
1½ cups flour
1 teaspoon baking powder
½ teaspoon ground cinnamon
¼ teaspoon ground nutmeg
⅛ teaspoon salt
½ cup milk
½ cup finely chopped hazelnuts

chocolate–rum icing
1 tablespoon egg white
1 cup confectioners' sugar
1 tablespoon cocoa
1½ tablespoons rum

Grease and flour 9 × 5 × 3-inch loaf pan; set aside.

Peel potato; coarsely grate. Place in tea towel; squeeze dry. There should be ¾ cup potato. Set aside.

Grate chocolate; set aside.

Cream butter and sugar until light. Add eggs and vanilla; beat well.

Sift together flour, baking powder, spices, and salt. Add alternately with milk to creamed mixture. Add potato, chocolate, and nuts; mix well. Turn into prepared loaf pan. Bake in preheated 350°F oven 55 minutes or until cake tests done. Cool cake in pan 30 minutes; turn out onto wire rack. Ice cake while still warm.

Beat egg white in small bowl with fork until foamy. Add confectioners' sugar, cocoa, and rum; stir until smooth. Spread over cake. Makes 6 servings.

potato rolls

1 medium potato, peeled, diced
1½ cups water
1 package active dry yeast
4 tablespoons sugar
½ cup hydrogenated vegetable shortening
2 eggs
1½ teaspoons salt
4 to 4½ cups all-purpose flour

Place potato and water in small saucepan; cover. Bring to boil. Reduce heat to low; cook approximately 10 minutes or until potato is tender. Drain; reserve potato water. (There should be 1 cup.) Steam potato in saucepan until dry. Mash without added ingredients. (There should be ½ cup.)

When potato water is lukewarm, pour into mixing bowl; add yeast. Stir until dissolved. Add mashed potato, sugar, shortening, eggs, salt, and 2 cups flour. Beat on low 1 minute, scraping bowl frequently. Increase speed to medium; beat 2 minutes. Mix in enough of remaining flour to make dough that can be easily handled. Turn out onto floured board; knead until dough is smooth and elastic. Place in greased bowl; rotate dough to grease surface. Cover; let rise in warm place until double in bulk.

Punch down dough; place on floured board. Flour surface of dough; divide into 16 rolls. Place in greased 10 × 10-inch-square pan. Cover; let stand in warm place until double in bulk.

Bake in 375°F oven 20 to 25 minutes, until golden and sounds hollow when tapped. Remove from pan.

Serve rolls hot with plenty of butter. Makes 16 large or 20 smaller rolls.

variation
1 tablespoon caraway seed can be added to dough with last addition of flour.

Note: Alternately, dough can be cut into 20 rolls and placed in 11 × 7-inch baking dish, following above directions.

plum jam

6 cups purple plums, quartered, stones removed
1 cup water
4 cups sugar
1 tablespoon lemon juice

Combine fruit and water in heavy enamel or stainless-steel pan. Bring to boil. Reduce heat to low; cook until fruit is tender.

Meanwhile, measure sugar into bowl; set to warm near pilot light, or place in electric oven and set temperature on warm. Leave element on 3 minutes; turn off. Leave sugar in oven until ready for use.

When fruit is tender, add sugar and lemon juice; stir until sugar is dissolved. Increase heat; boil 30 minutes, stirring to prevent burning, or until mixture jells when tested on cold saucer. Pour into hot sterilized jars; seal. Makes 6 cups.

irish fry

2 cups peeled, diced apples, pears, peaches, or plums or a mixture
   of these
3 tablespoons Irish whiskey
2 egg yolks
⅔ cup flat beer
1 tablespoon melted butter or margarine
1 cup all-purpose flour
¼ teaspoon salt
1 tablespoon sugar
2 egg whites
Oil for deep frying
Confectioners' sugar

Combine diced fruit and whiskey; mix well. Let stand while preparing batter.

Beat egg yolks, beer, and butter together. Add dry ingredients; beat until no lumps remain. Cover; refrigerate 2 hours.

Drain fruit well; mix with batter.

Whip egg whites until stiff but not dry. Fold into fritter batter lightly but thoroughly.

Meanwhile, heat 3 inches oil in deep fryer to 375°F. Drop batter by tablespoons into hot oil; cook until golden (3 to 4 minutes). Drain on absorbent paper. Dust with confectioners' sugar. Serve immediately. Makes 6 servings.

index